Ee Ff Gg

Mm Nn Oo Pp

Vv Ww Xx

Cc Dd Ee Ff

Kk Ll Mm

Caroline Perkins
Illustrated by Valerie Delgado

ABC get to know the SAiNTS with me!

Irondale, Alabama

Cover and interior design by Perceptions Design Studio.

EWTN Publishing, Inc.
5817 Old Leeds Road, Irondale, AL 35210

Distributed by Sophia Institute Press, Box 5284, Manchester, NH 03108.

ISBN: 978-1-68278-101-2
Library of Congress Control Number: 2020945325

Third Printing

This book is dedicated to Jack
& our favorite saints.

—CAROLINE PERKINS

is for Anthony
for when things are lost.

Bb

is for Benedict
fighting evil at all cost.

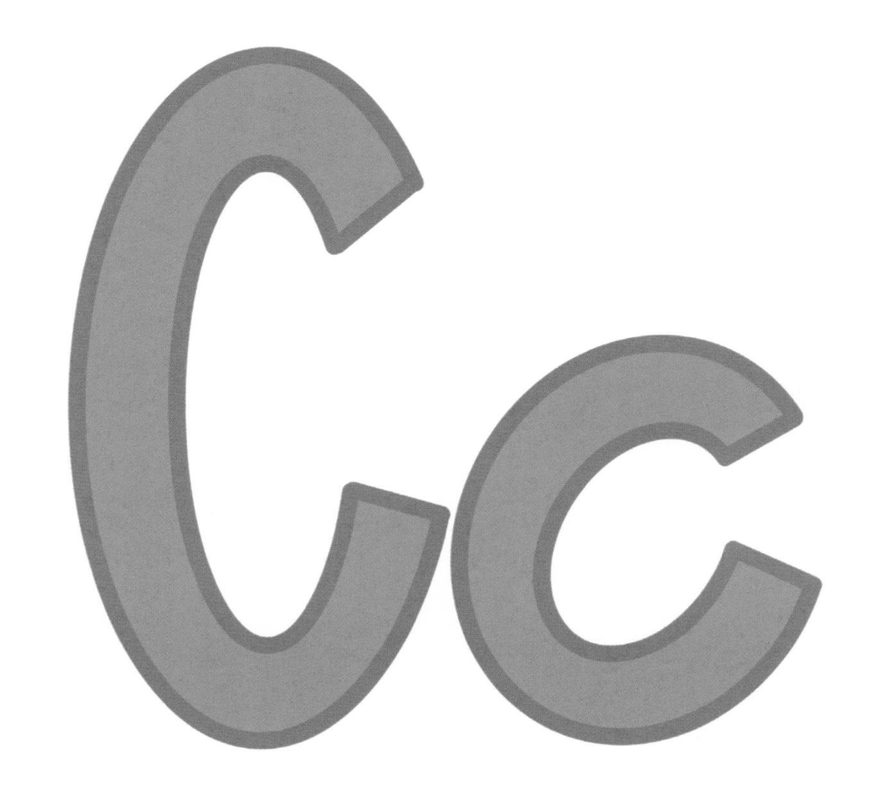

is for Christopher
on adventures far and wide.

is for Dymphna
when feeling hopeless inside.

Ee

is for Elizabeth Ann Seton,
a teacher in the USA.

JESUS
loves
you!

is for Faustina
spreading the Divine Mercy way.

is for Gerard.

He protects the small.

is for hermits. The first one was Paul. He lived in a cave with no one at all.

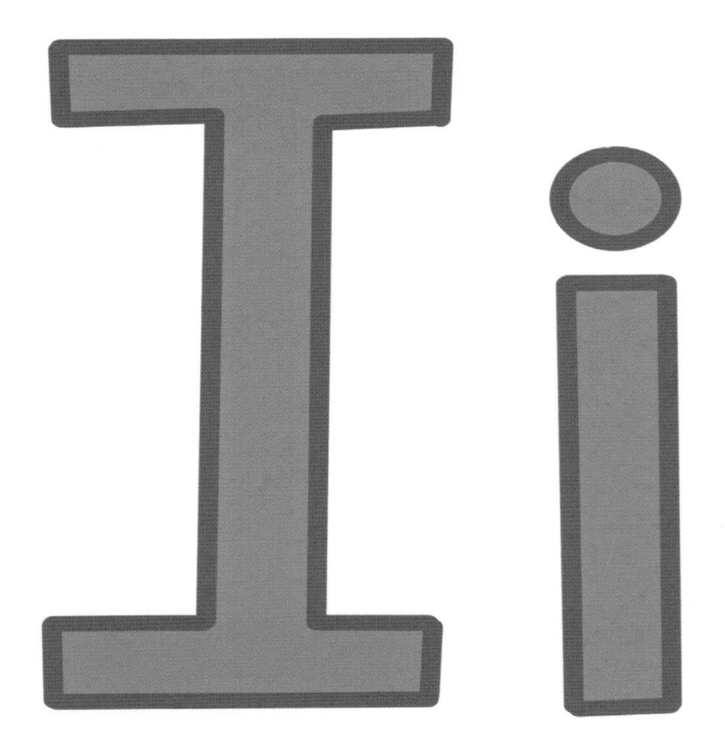

is for Ignatius
providing spiritual aid.

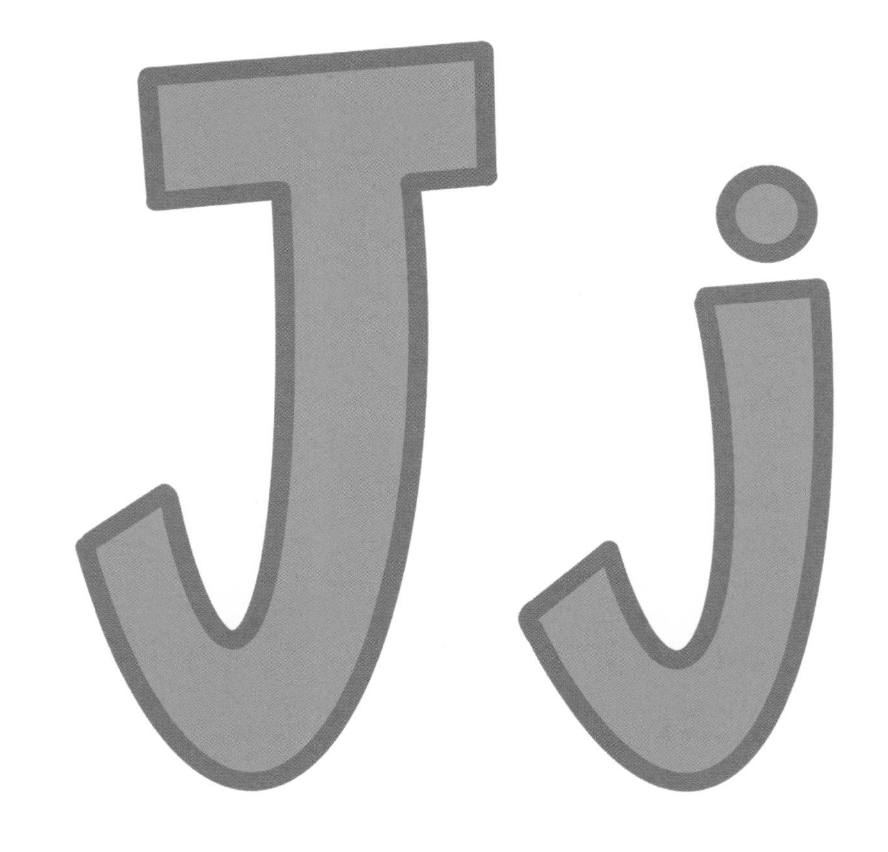

is for John Paul II saying,

“Be not afraid.”

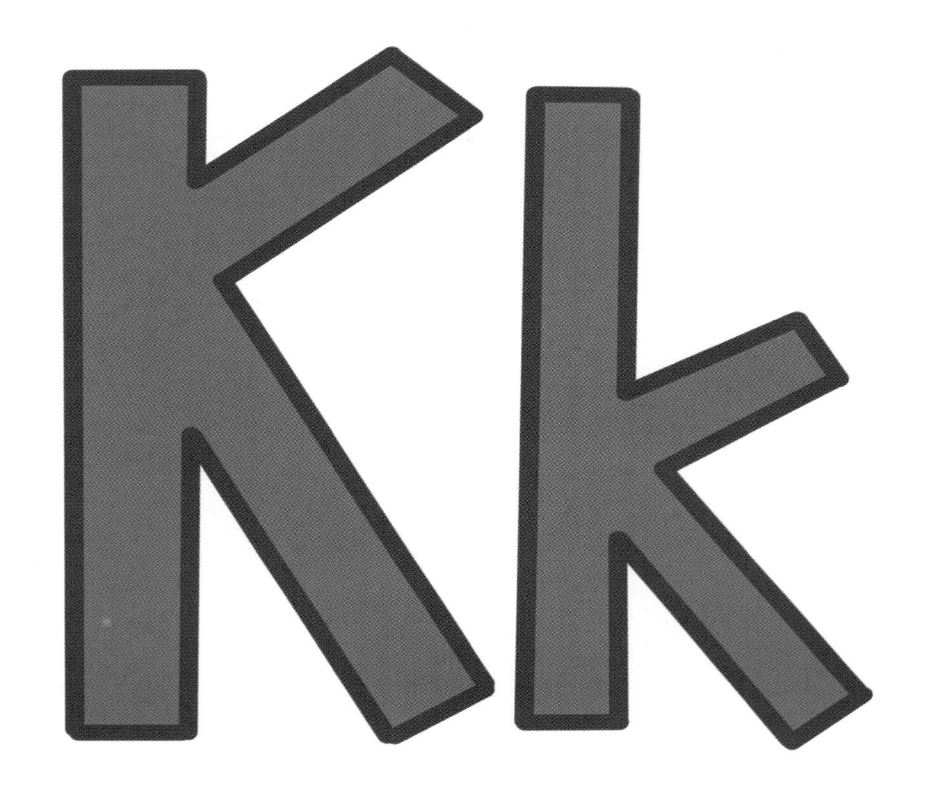

is for Kateri
protecting the earth
where we live.

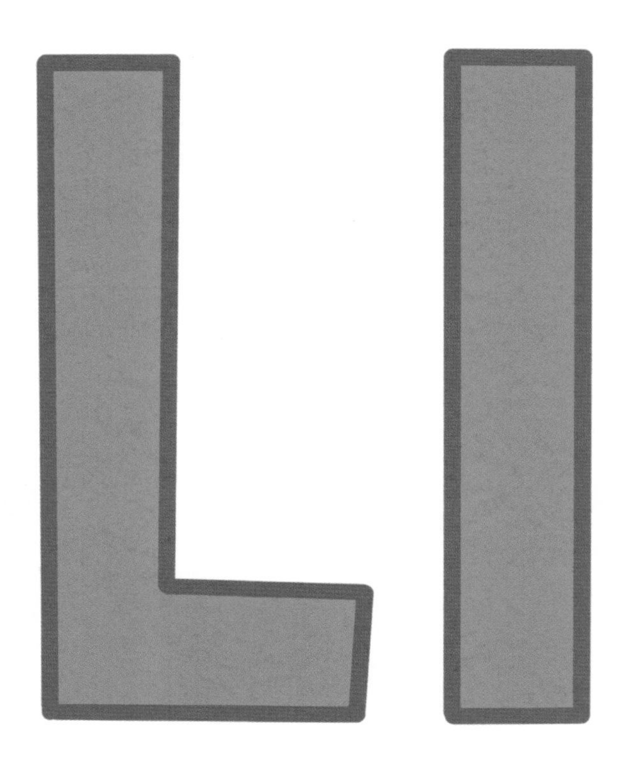

is for Luke
sharing Jesus' message
to forgive.

LUKE 17:4
AND IF HE
WRONGS YOU
EVEN TIMES IN
ONE DAY AND
RETURNS TO YOU
'I AM
SORRY."
YOU
SHOULD
FORGIVE
HIM."

is for martyrs like
Matthew and Maximilian.

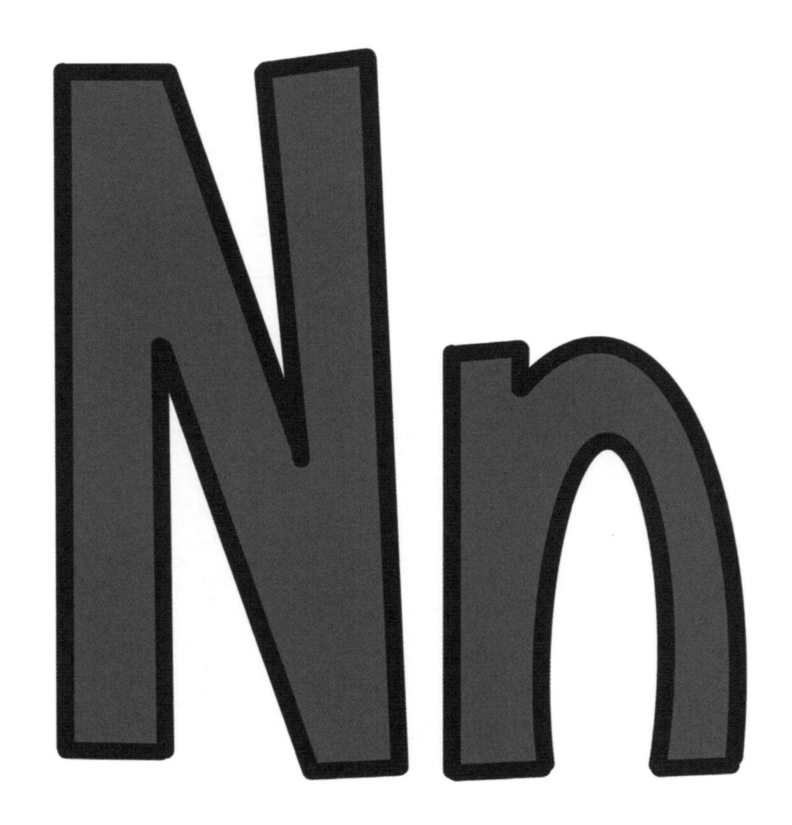

is for Nicholas
giving gifts to poor children.

DECEMBER

6

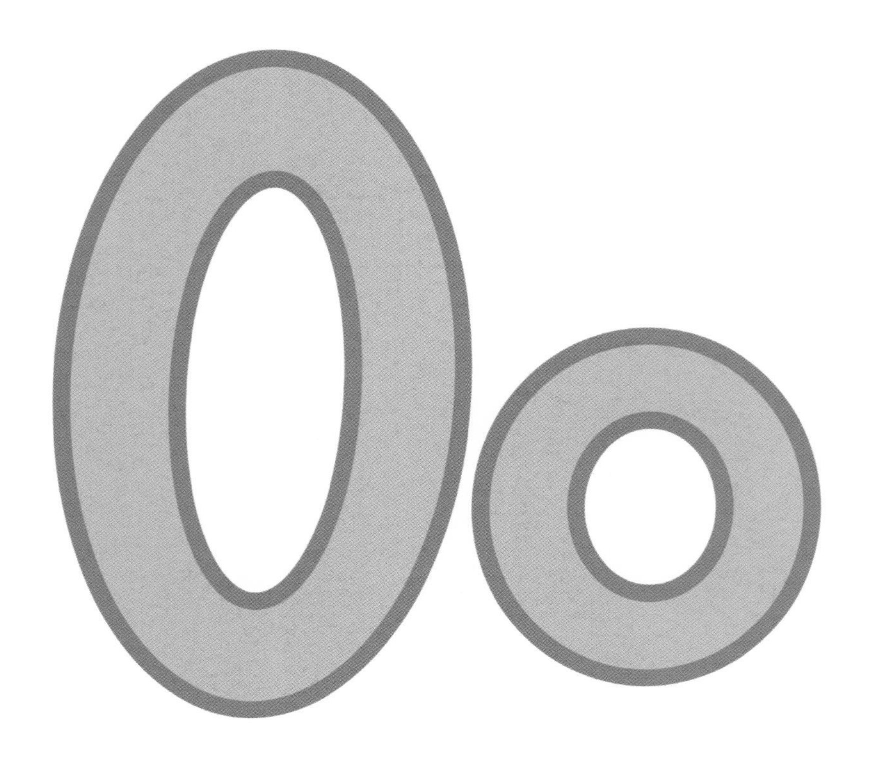

is for Our Lady and the
love that she shares.

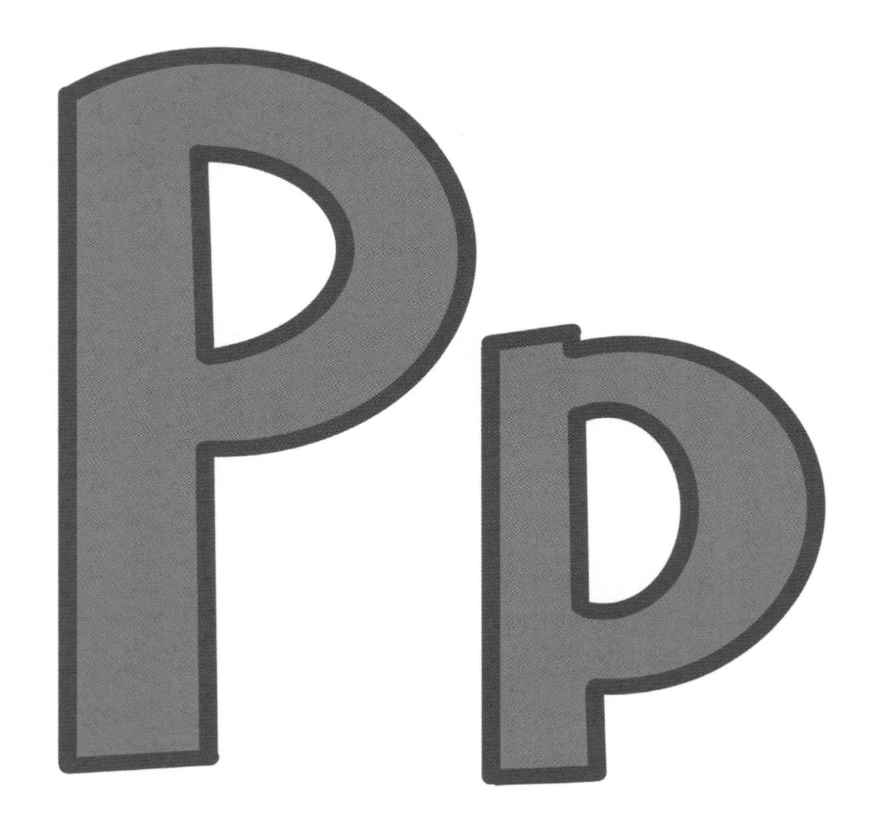

is for Padre Pio
and his powerful prayers.

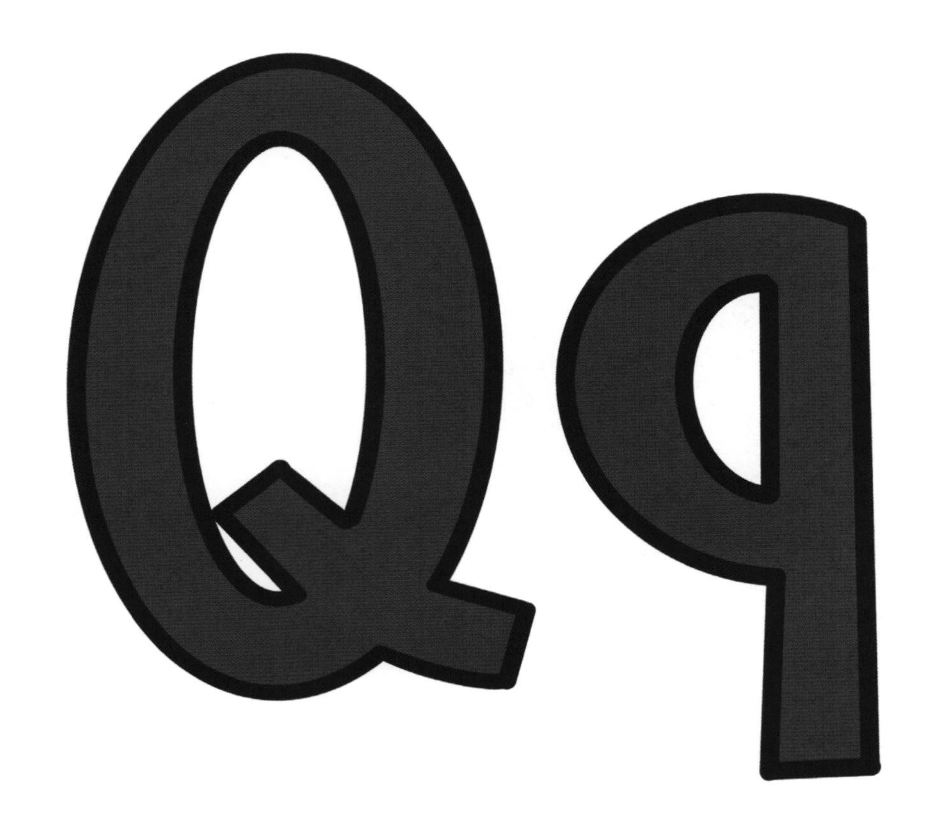

is for quiet ones like Joseph
and John the Silent.

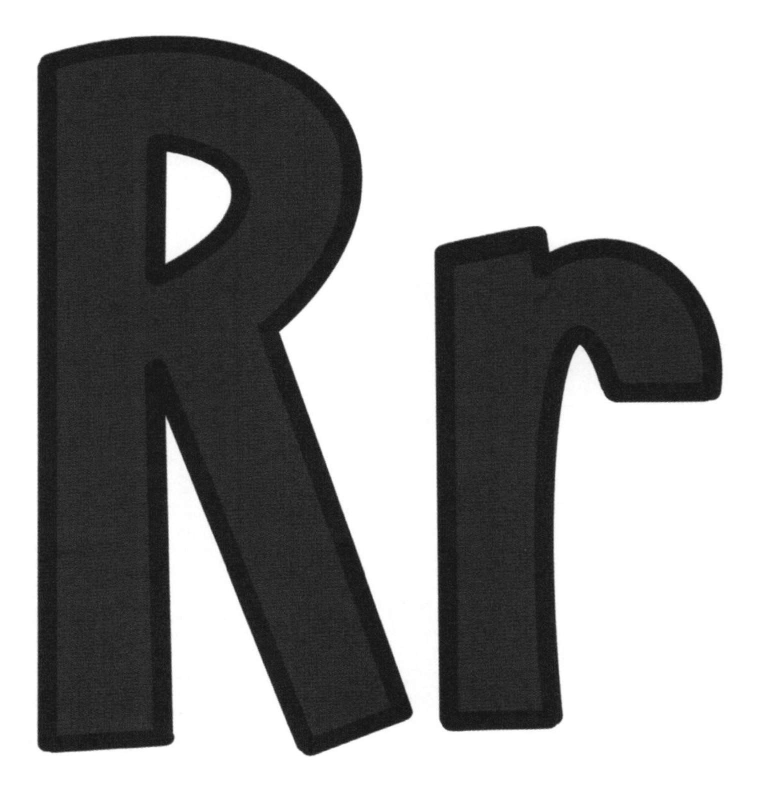

is for Rose.

Her beauty is vibrant.

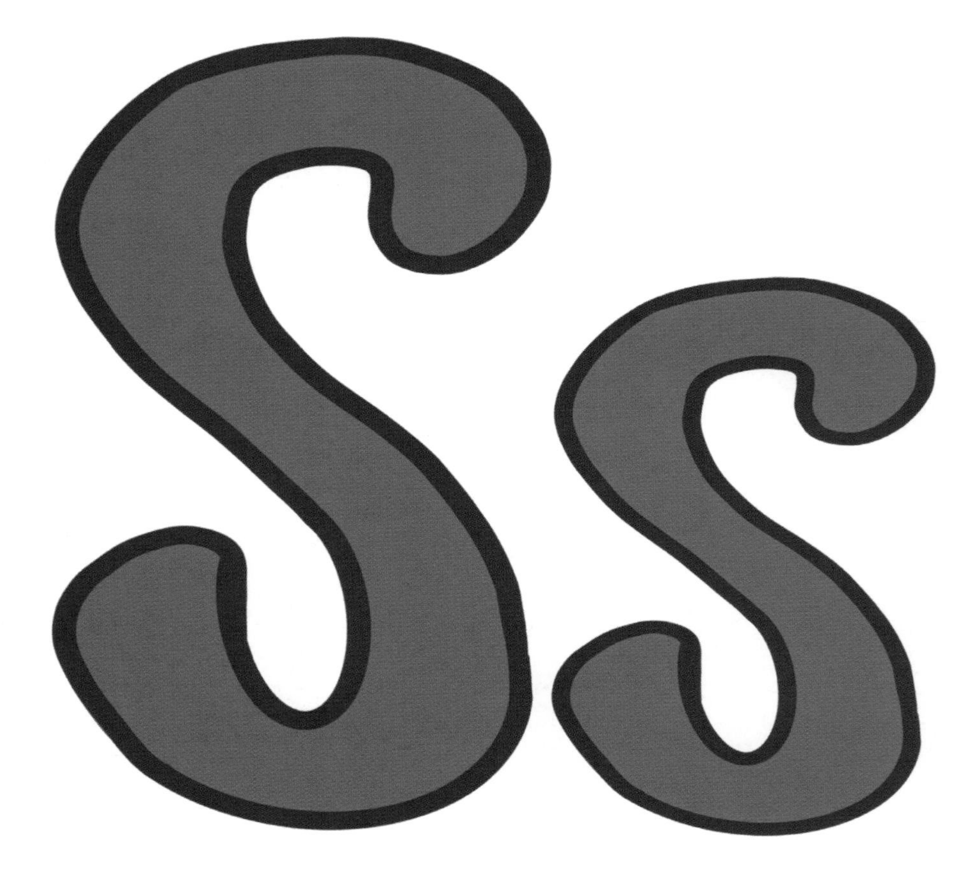

is for Simon
carrying Jesus' Cross that day.

is for Thérèse

and her "Little Way" to pray.

is for Ursula
serving the Lord with grace.

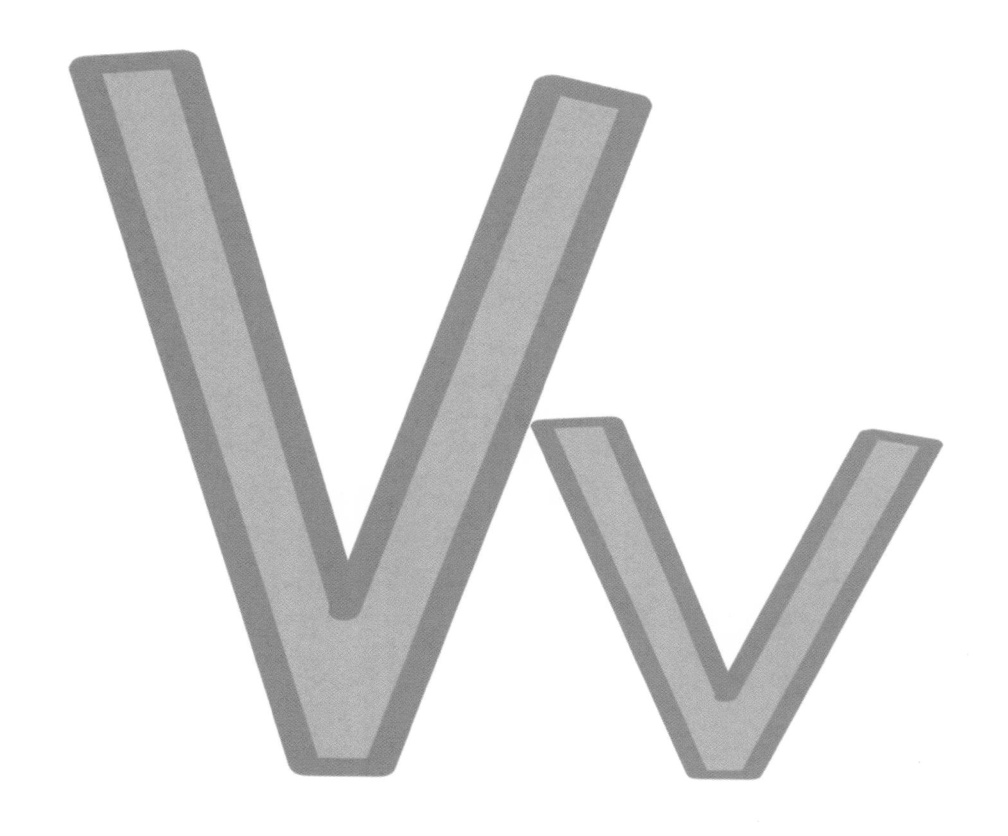

is for Veronica
wiping Jesus' face.

is for Walburga,
a friend of sailors at sea.

is for Xantippa.
Her life is a mystery.

is for YOU.

You can be a saint too.

is for ZOOOM.
Now you're on your way!
Jesus and your new saint
friends can help you each day.

Be not afraid!

Aa Bb Cc Dd

Ii Jj Kk Ll

Qq Rr Ss Tt

Yy Zz Aa Bb

Gg Hh Ii Jj